House Cleaning Tips

How to Clean and Declutter Your Home Fast

Sherrie Le Masurier

Disclaimer

By reading this book, you assume all risks associated with using the advice given below, with a full understanding that you, solely, are responsible for anything that may occur as a result of putting this information into action in any way, and regardless of your interpretation of the advice.

House Cleaning Tips

How to Clean and Declutter Your Home Fast

Table of Contents

Introduction

Do you enjoy housecleaning? The truth is most of us don't. While some people find it relaxing and actually enjoy the process of decluttering and cleaning stuff, most of us just like the end result. Windows we can see out of, stainless steel sinks that shine and the smell of our home when everything is freshly cleaned.

Clearing out the clutter *(and the dust bunnies)* doesn't have to be a chore. Over the years, I've discovered a few tips and techniques for how to declutter your home and how to clean it fast so you can get onto more enjoyable things.

Along the way, I've also discovered that the process of decluttering and house cleaning really isn't as bad as I

first thought. With the right tools, techniques and products, I've even come to enjoy it. While maybe it isn't as
fun as taking the day off to do something I really like
but there certainly is a lot of satisfaction in a job well
done, especially when you have some good maintenance
tips up your sleeve.

Speaking of maintenance, I turned over a new leaf last
year and switched from doing a traditional spring clean,
to more of year-round house clean.

You see, when I initially set out on my mission to find
quicker more efficient ways to attack my spring cleaning
ritual and discovered store shelves lined with countless
products to whiten, brighten, unclog and disinfect, I
thought what's the point of doing an annual out and out
spring clean when I can easily *(and routinely)* clean as
we transition from season to season?

Now I'm in the habit of decluttering regularly and main-
taining our home with daily, weekly, monthly and
seasonal cleaning and organizing routines.

That said, while I no longer face a big cleaning session
when the warmer weather hits, I do find the first signs of
spring motivating for opening up our windows and fresh-
ening our home as well as giving it a facelift with a fresh
coat of paint, new organizers and/or seasonal flowers.

So whether you prefer doing a big spring clean or going
the house cleaning maintenance route throughout the
year, I've got some helpful tips and techniques to share.

How to Declutter

For many of us, the most overwhelming part of cleaning our home is getting rid of the clutter. There's no two ways around it, decluttering your home can be a huge job.

Cleaning with any efficiency is almost impossible if you have to keep stopping to pick stuff up. You know the kind of stuff I'm referring to - newspapers, dirty clothes, towels, toys etc.

If you're really determined to conquer some clutter, be sure to allot enough time to tackle it from start to finish.

If you only have an afternoon, consider spending it on a project like cleaning out the clutter from the front closet.

A whole weekend is more practical for tackling the basement or garage. Regardless of what task you undertake, make sure you can accomplish more than just taking everything out and leaving a big mess.

When it comes to clearing clutter, there are positive and negative approaches to decluttering your home.

The worst way to approach your clutter is to grab a box or garbage bag and out of disgust and frustration, get rid of everything lying around.

The positive way to declutter is to evaluate each item before you get rid of it.

3 Questions You Need To Answer

If you're unsure as to whether an item should stay or go, you need to ask yourself the following three questions:

Do I use it?

Do I need it?

Do I REALLY want it?

If your answer is no, eliminate it! Pass along unwanted items by giving away or selling via a consignment store or yard sale.

To simplify the decluttering process grab a marker and four pieces of paper and write 'Keep', 'Give Away', 'Relocate', and 'Trash'.

These are the four ways you'll categorize your items. Now grab and label either four individual laundry baskets or boxes *(or just spread the category headings on your floor)* and get started.

Note: You can always take a break later and run to your local grocery store for the appropriate number of boxes (you may actually need more than four).

Decluttering Tips

Following are basic techniques on how to declutter your home quickly and help you shave a ton of time off the cleaning process.

First and foremost, come up with a focused plan of attack that is realistic and works within your existing schedule e.g. plan weekly one to two hour decluttering sessions each week or do a top-to-bottom declutter one weekend.

The latter may be unrealistic while the former should be much more manageable. Get the whole family involved and soon you'll find satisfaction in accomplishing things one step at a time.

That said for immediate results, you can do a quick clean sweep of the surface clutter around your home and start sorting it.

Personally, I favor breaking things down and doing a serious decluttering one room at a time over several days.

The positive effects of the latter option will be longer lasting if you also take the time to work your way through the closets, cupboards and drawers in each room.

Purging unwanted items is only the first step. The second is to find an appropriate home for any items you want to keep.

Once you've decluttered your home of unnecessary items, and have begun the process of visualizing a proper storage place for 'necessary' items, you'll have a realistic sense of just how much storage space you have.

There's one final step to take before we move onto home storage solutions and that is to remove everything from your home that didn't make it into your 'Keep' category.

If you're donating the items in your 'Give Away' box, take everything out to your car and make a plan to drop by a Goodwill or Salvation Army store in the next day or two. Or pass the items along to a friend or neighbour ASAP.

Any items to be relocated can remain boxed up for now. Just put the box or boxes somewhere out of the way until after you've cleaned and you have the proper storage containers to house them.

Home Storage Solutions

When it comes to home storage, setting some priorities as to what goes where is beneficial. Keep frequently used items readily accessible. If you have young children, you'll want to ensure they can access the items they need themselves. Likewise, infrequently used items are most appropriate for high shelves or remote nooks and crannies.

Now for the best ways to contain your stuff, your options range from bins, baskets, hooks and mini-shelves. The key is to make the most of your available space. Where possible, your storage items should be clearly visible or boxed and labelled. You'll also want a flexible storage system that can be adapted to your changing needs.

Store like things together

When you categorize items into groups of like things, it's much easier to find what you need right away, eliminating the need to hunt all over for related items. For example, a pocket organizer hung on the back of your hall closet door will keep sunscreen, sunglasses, swim goggles, ear plugs, bathing caps and the like in one main location. Likewise, keeping snack foods together and storing all your baking ingredients on its own shelf is beneficial in your pantry.

Make the most of vertical space

Stacking bins are great for maximizing space especially ones with slide-out drawers.

Moveable storage

You can't beat a rolling cart for easy access. Simply roll out the cart when you need it and store it away in a closet or under a table when you don't.

Open storage

If you have an open storage shelf your best bet is to co-ordinate your storage containers with your decor e.g. wicker baskets in your family room or colorful plastic bins in your child's bedroom.

Be creative

Think outside the box when it comes to home storage solutions e.g. use cutlery and ice cube trays for keeping things organized and for storing small items elsewhere in your home or garage.

Organizing Your Home

Entrance Know How

Create an organized area by the door you use most often. Find a nearby home for everything that usually ends up in a pile on the floor. Consider adult and child-sized hooks positioned at appropriate heights. If you have room, supply a bench for putting on shoes and boots and for storing *(on the shelf beneath)* hats, gloves and other outdoor gear in labeled bins.

If you have a wall side table use it wisely by utilizing its' drawers for keys, keeping baskets of incoming and outgoing mail, and as place for library books and borrowed items needing to returned.

Keep a mini recycling bin handy to toss junk mail into at first sight. Otherwise, it will just add to the clutter.

You may also want to include a few decorative boxes with lids for items you frequently take with you when you leave the house. Boxes with lids also make hiding things much easier when company unexpectedly comes over.

Keeping your cellphone charger nearby your most frequented door is great for forming the habit of automatically charging it when you get home and increases the chance you'll also remember it on your way out.

If you have room in your hall closet, store a 'Give Away' box. Toss in any and everything you find is cluttering up your home and you want to get rid of. When the box is full, make the decision to quickly go through it and decide where the items will go – to charity, to friends, or to be boxed up and stored elsewhere for your next yard sale. Better yet, don't even go through it, just seal up the box and deposit it at a local charitable drop-off center.

Making the Most of Your Kitchen

If you have space in your kitchen, consider creating a combined office/home information center, where you can pay bills, make phone calls and keep files. A nearby calendar and a memo board will also go a long way to helping you keep on top of things.

If space is a real issue, think about getting a rolling file cart you can store in a nearby closet or using a series of portable file boxes for different subjects.

Give each family member their own in-box for phone messages, mail and other papers.

Plastic trays of different shapes and sizes make short work of decluttering your junk drawer.

Devise a master shopping list of the items you usually buy, make copies and keep one posted on the fridge. Encourage family members to get in the habit of checking off foods as they are consumed.

Stacking bins on wheels are also an excellent storage tool for supplies if your child uses the kitchen table for homework and/or art projects.

Simplifying Shared Spaces

When everyone takes a few minutes to pick up after themselves, you eliminate the frustration of having to do everything yourself. Consider making a family rule that everyone is responsible for putting away their own stuff. Anything left out after bedtime gets put in a lost-and-found box in the hallway. A note to the wise, make a point to go through the box once a week.

Bathroom Storage and Organizing

Assign family members their own color for towels, wash-cloths and toothbrushes. Storing personal toiletry bags or bins under the sink is also a good way to keep every-one's stuff organized.

Linen Closet Organization

Create individual piles of bedding and towels. Store each complete set of sheets in one of the coordinating pillow-cases.

Laundry Room Sorting

Separate whites and colors by using two hampers or laundry baskets, or use the divided kind and make sure everyone has their own. Make your kids responsible for delivering their dirty clothes to the laundry room on speci-fied laundry days.

A smaller basket stored nearby your laundry or bath tub is handy for hand washables. If you have an extra plastic

salad spinner, store it close by to make short work of hand washing delicates. Or simply wash out your panty hose or lingerie the next time you shower.

Maintenance Routines

Even if you're super busy, regular routines and mainte-nance isn't as difficult as it may seem, the key is to find the time, make a commitment, and stick to it.

Carve out extra time in your day by subtracting even as little as 15 minutes from daily activities that aren't as im-portant e.g. limit your TV viewing or Internet surfing time.

The following are some of my favorite maintenance and routine tips:

Do a 15 minute sweep of your home

A daily 15 minutes should be all that it takes to reclaim order in your home. Give yourself a solid 15 minutes when you get home from work or right after the kids go to bed and do a quick sweep of each room. Pick up and tidy as you go. The key here is to deal with any visible clutter as you move from room to room. Don't stay in any one spot for long, simply give momentary attention to the things that need it and move on.

Make sweeping or 'Swiffering' part of your daily routine

Whether you have laminate floors, ceramic, hardwood or carpet floors a quick daily sweep or 'Swiffer' will keep the dirt, dust bunnies and pet hair at bay. Add the couple of extra minutes it takes to clean floors, to the end of your meal time clean up routine.

Routinely clean your sinks

Whenever you use a sink whether it's to wash dishes or to brush your teeth, clean it right after. Like routinely making your bed, your kitchen and bathrooms will look cleaner and tidier when you take the moment or two necessary to shine up the kitchen sink so you can see your reflection or wipe up the remains of your favorite toothpaste.

When you make a mess, clean it up

Just like clutter breeds more clutter so does a mess. If you make a mess, clean it up right away, otherwise you may end up with a real disaster on your hands. I know we're busy as parents but we need to lead by example, if we take something out we need to put it back when we're finished with it. If we don't, what does that teach our kids when we tell them to put away the toy they're playing with before taking out another one?

Incorporate storage into your decor

Don't overdo your decor. Less can often be more. Too many things can weigh you down. In other words, 'more' means maintenance. Eliminate as much visual decor as possible that needs dusting and instead opt for colorful baskets and bins that match your decor. When shopping for new furniture consider multi-functional styles like storage ottomans, end tables with a drawer and shelves, and bookcase headboards.

Multi-task when it makes sense

Waiting for the kettle to boil? Wash up a few dishes or load the dishwasher. Or take a few minutes to wipe the interior and exterior of your kitchen cabinets down when you put your dishes away.

Give new things a home

Never buy anything unless you need it, but when you do, always give it a home right away. Otherwise, it will contribute to the clutter you're trying to get rid of.

Avoid the temptation to just put things anywhere

Take the moment or two it takes to put things away in their proper place.

Build on what's working

Once you've found success with a particular organizing system or strategy, consider tweaking it and repeating it elsewhere.

House Cleaning 101

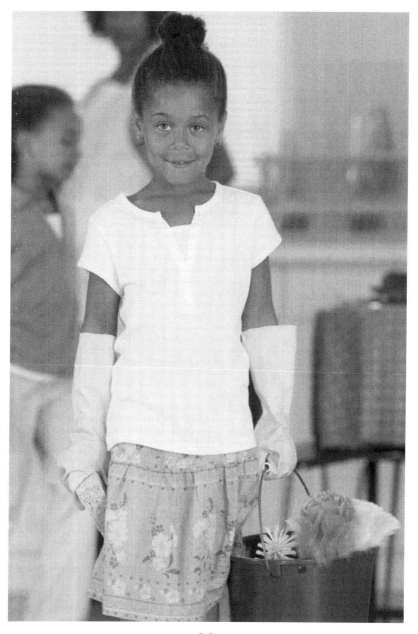

There are certain things you should do before you get started, the first of which is get some help. Enlist the help of your significant other and your kids. The theory is if you teach children to help out when they're young, they see cleaning as more of a habit than a chore.

Next you'll want to assemble all your supplies. Grab everything you're going to need before you get started. And, just because a cleaner smells strong doesn't mean it will clean better. A good mild-formula general purpose glass and counter cleaner will handle most of your cleaning needs.

Here are some more things to consider prior to starting your house cleaning project.

Put On Some Music

Clean to some of your favorite tunes. It makes the process of cleaning more fun.

Remove Obstacles

Temporarily relocate all small appliances, knickknacks and other items from the tops of counters and dressers to one central location.

Ease Into It

Start with an easy task. Seeing quick results helps motivate.

Keep Distractions to a Minimum

Put your phone on voice mail and make sure young kids are busy with an age appropriate task *(or activity)* of their own.

If It Isn't Dirty, Don't Clean It

Consider spot cleaning instead of cleaning the whole thing just because of a tiny smudge.

Work Together

Leaving wastebaskets outside of the rooms being cleaned increases the chances of having them emptied all at once. Likewise, consider leaving the vacuum handy for the next user.

One Room at a Time

Jumping between rooms can cost you valuable time organizing and reorganizing yourself.

Start in the Corner

Many cleaning professionals recommend you start in the corner of the room farthest from the door and work your way around. No more retracing your steps.

Dust from Top to Bottom

Since dirt settles downward always start dusting at the top.

Use a Two Bucket Method

Implement a two bucket or a divided bucket system *(soapy water and clean water)* when cleaning surfaces that need rinsing.

Let Cleansers Do the Dirty Work

Save time and energy scrubbing by spraying on cleansers and leaving them to work away while you work on another nearby task. That way, the loosening and the dissolving of the dirt will be done for you and you can wipe it away more efficiently.

Vacuum Last

When you leave vacuuming to the last you don't have to worry about wiping crumbs onto the floor when dusting. Attach a long extension cord so you don't have to continually unplug and re-plug the vacuum. Make the most of your vacuum attachments to dust blinds, lampshades, throw pillows etc.

Spring Cleaning Checklist

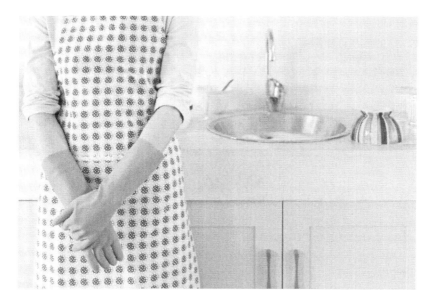

Here`s an overview of what needs to be addressed throughout the house. The following spring cleaning checklist explains the basic techniques required to help you clean virtually every surface or object in your home.

Highlight or check off each as task as you complete it.

Clean walls and ceilings

Use a vacuum to remove dust then tackle stubborn surface grime.

Reseal grout

Protect the cement-based material between household titles with a penetrating grout sealer. A small foam brush works best on the porous surface.

Vacuum and shampoo your carpets

You can easily deep clean synthetic carpets and rugs *(with waterproof backings)* yourself using a rotary shampooer and a hot water extraction machine. Rugs without backing should be left to professional cleaners.

Wax non-wood floors

Restore the shine to vinyl and linoleum floors by waxing with a polish designed specifically for these surfaces. Additionally bring the shine back to stone and tile floors with either a paste or liquid wax designed for the particular material.

Clean upholstery

Remove cushions and vacuum furniture with upholstery and crevice tools. Gently beat cushions by hand outdoors to remove dust. Address stains only after reading the care labels.

Dust books and shelves

Take all the books off your shelves and dust both before reassembling. A dust brush or crevice tool attached to your vacuum will let you get into all those tight spots. Use a clean, soft cloth to wipe down leather-bound books.

Give your home a thorough dust

It's that time of year when you need to get into those hard-to-reach places and often neglected spots like the top of ceiling fans and window casings. Give everything the once over with a feather duster. Start at the top of the room and work your way down. Finish up by vacuuming the dust that settles on the floor.

Wax wood furniture

Wood surfaces are best cleaned with a soft cloth dampened with water and a mild dishwashing liquid prior to applying a paste wax with a cotton rag. Once the wax dries, buff with a clean cloth.

Clean window treatments

Always check care labels before machine washing any fabric window treatments. Fabric shades are usually best dry cleaned. Use only a damp cloth on wood blinds. Dust metal and vinyl blinds and then add a little mild dishwashing liquid to a bucket of warm water and clean with a soft cloth or sponge.

Wash window screens

Use a scrub brush along with laundry detergent or a dishwashing liquid to clean your window screens. Rinse in a bathtub or outdoors with a garden hose.

Polish window and door hardware

Medium tarnished hardware is best cleaned with liquid polishes and polish-impregnated cloths whereas heavy tarnished hardware responds better to pastes and creams.

How to Clean

There are many different types of cleaning jobs people consider the worst. They range from cleaning a chandelier to dealing with thawed freezer contents in the aftermath of an electrical failure. But behind every cleaning chore, I believe there is creative solution. For instance, baby oil does a great job of shining stainless steel and dulled porcelain.

The following are creative solutions to some tough but common cleaning chores:

In The Kitchen

Dishwashers

To rid any food discoloration, fill the detergent cup with orange drink crystals and run for a complete *(but dish free)* cycle.

High Chairs

Put your food splattered high chair in the shower or take it outside. Use a soapy sponge or scrub it down with a brush. Then turn on the shower or spray with the garden hose.

Grease Splattered Walls

Clean grease off walls by blotting first with a paper towel then sprinkle a little cornstarch on a cloth, and apply until no more cornstarch can be absorbed. Wipe off to clean.

Freezer Odor

Combat smelly freezers with a pie plate full of used coffee grounds. Let stand for a couple of days until the odor disappears.

In The Bathroom

Double Your Cleaning Power

Clean your bathroom fixtures and your hair brushes *(re-move excess hair first)* at the same time by laying them in the sink and giving everything a spray with a foaming bathroom cleaner. Rinse thoroughly and let dry.

Shower Curtains

Don't toss out your shower curtain just because of a little soap scum. Launder it in your washing machine in warm water to which one half cup each of detergent and baking soda has been added. Include two large bath towels in the cycle to help clean off the soap scum. Add 1 cup of vinegar to the rinse water. Don't wash out the vinegar. Hang to dry.

Shower Tiles

Start by running a very hot shower for two to three minutes then wash the tile with a mixture of one half cup ammonia, one half cup white vinegar, one quarter cup washing soda and one liter of water. For major stains, scrub with a paste of three parts baking soda and one part bleach.

Bathmats

Use the same technique for cleaning rubber or vinyl bathmats as suggested for cleaning shower curtains. Just don't forget the towels since they actively work at scrubbing the mat for you.

Toilet Bowls

Clean stained toilet bowels by dropping in a denture tablet or pouring in some cola.

Around The House

Mini Blinds

The best way, I've found to clean mini blinds other than regularly vacuuming is to soak them in ammonia, rinse and then hang them over a clothesline, shower curtain rod or fence. You could also take them to a do-it-yourself car wash and hose them down.

Hard To Reach Cleaning

Slip an old sock over the end of a broom *handle (remove the broom part first)* and secure with a rubber band. This will help you clean behind furniture and other places you can't normally reach.

Artificial Flowers

Place your artificial flowers in a paper bag along with a handful of salt. Close tightly and shake for a couple of minutes. The salt will attract any dust and dirt.

Knickknacks

Use a blow dryer and a fine paintbrush to dust your knickknacks. Also consider wiping them with a damp fabric softener sheet to help reduce static which attracts dust. *(The same 'anti- static' technique can also be used on your blinds.)*

Chandeliers

Combine two teaspoons of rubbing alcohol and one cup of warm water in a spray bottle. Hang an umbrella upside down from the chandelier to catch the drips then spray away.

Cleaning Wallpaper

To clean soiled non-washable wallpaper, rub gently with an art gum eraser or a crust-less slice of bread.

Sliding Door Tracks

Using all-purpose cleaner, spray the track and let it soak for a couple of minutes. Wipe out the loosened dirt with a paper towel. Place a cleaning cloth over a flat screwdriver blade and run it up and down the track until clean. Now run the door back and forth a few times to clean the glides.

Windows

To easily tell which side of the window the streaks are on, use vertical strokes when washing outside and horizontal strokes when washing inside.

Baking Soda
& Vinegar

Baking soda and vinegar is a staple in most kitchens but are you maximizing their full potential?

Inexpensive and environmentally-friendly, you can't beat the cleaning, disinfecting and deodorizing properties of these two multi-purpose natural products especially when it comes to keeping your kitchen safe and spotless.

Baking soda is a must have in your kitchen whether you bake or not. In addition to playing an active role in baking, a simple box of baking soda does a multitude of things from deodorizing your refrigerator to smothering grease fires.

White distilled vinegar is also an excellent cleaner for all kitchen surfaces including counters, refrigerators and stove tops.

Before we get into the many cleaning properties of baking soda and vinegar, I'm going to explain what they are and what makes them so versatile.

What is baking soda?

Baking soda *(also referred to as 'bicarbonate of soda')* is a sodium bicarbonate, a natural substance that maintains its' pH balance. Since it has the ability to neutralize acids and bases, baking soda actually eliminates odors instead of simply covering them up.

When heated, baking soda releases carbon dioxide which in turn causes baked goods to rise.

Additionally baking soda offers very mild abrasive properties making it an ideal cleaner for everything from sinks and counter tops, to the removal of stains from fine china.

What is vinegar?

Vinegar is a weak form of acetic acid that forms through the fermentation of sugars or starches. Due to its level of acidity it is also effective for killing mold, bacteria, and germs.

For the purposes of cleaning, it's best to use white distilled vinegar at 100% concentration.

In addition to your regular jug of vinegar, every kitchen can benefit from at least one spray bottle of vinegar. I personally like to have one spray bottle of pure white vinegar and another one mixed 50/50 with water. Keeping my spray bottles handy really makes efficient work of cleaning my kitchen.

Baking Soda Uses

REFRIGERATOR and FREEZER

One of the most common ways to use baking soda is to store an opened box of it in your refrigerator and freezer to help eliminate odors. For best results, replace the box every three months. A good habit to get into is to start a fresh box on the first day of each new season.

Wash Fridge/Freezer Interior

Eliminate any stale odors that linger by washing the interior of your fridge or freezer with baking soda and water every time you clean it out. Sprinkle a little baking soda in a pail of water.

Odor-Free Crisper

Eliminate odors in your crisper by sprinkling a little baking soda in its interior. Cover with a paper towel. Replace every three months.

Stain Removal

The best way to remove food and rust residue from your fridge interior is to make up a simple paste by adding a splash of water to a tablespoon or so of baking soda.

39

STOVE TOP and OVEN

Since baking soda causes dirt and grease to dissolve in water, you'll also find it to be a very effective cleaner for stove tops and ovens.

Clean Up Food Splatters

The best way to clean a messy stove top is to wet the area first *(a spray bottle of water works great)* and then sprinkle on some baking soda. Leave for an hour and then wipe clean. If the food splatters are really burnt on repeat and leave to sit overnight.

Oven Door

Sprinkle the inside of your oven door with baking soda and then rub with paper towels until all the grease is absorbed. If your door is especially greasy, sprinkle on a second round of baking soda and cover with a wet paper towel. Let sit for an hour or so before wiping the door clean with a damp cloth.

Major Oven Spills

Major oven spills are easy to clean up if you sprinkle them with baking soda when they're still fresh. Leave for a while and then remove with a sponge and some warm, soapy water.

Range Hood Filter

Immerse your wire mesh range hood filter in a pan of hot water. Pour on a little baking soda and watch as the grease floats away.

Oven Racks

Clean oven *(and BBQ grill)* racks by placing them in a garbage bag and taking them outside. Mix together 1 cup baking soda with ½ cup ammonia and pour in the bag. Tie the bag up with twist ties and leave outside until morning. The racks should easily wipe clean in the morning.

MICROWAVE

Cleaning the Inside

The interior of your microwave is best cleaned with a mixture of warm water and baking soda. Wipe down all the surfaces.

Eliminate Odors

Keep your microwave fresh by storing a pretty (microwave safe) dish or mug filled with baking soda inside it when it's not in use.

Tough Cleaning

For tough microwave cleaning jobs, boil some water with 2 tablespoons of baking soda in it. Allow to boil for several minutes. Any food particles should now be loosened and you can easily clean the interior with a sponge or paper towel.

DISHWASHER

No More Dishwasher Detergent?

Mix 2 tablespoons each of baking soda and borax together as a dishwasher detergent substitute.

Absorb Dishwasher Odors

If your dishwasher isn't full enough to be run, sprinkle on a little baking soda to absorb odors in the interim. When ready to run your dishwasher simply add your regular detergent to your second cycle dispenser *(the baking soda replaces the detergent normally used in the first cycle).*

Freshen Your Dishwasher

To freshen up a stale smelling dishwasher add ½ box of baking soda and put through a rinse cycle.

APPLIANCES

Shine Your Toaster Oven

A blend of baking soda and warm water does wonders for cleaning and shining the exterior of your toaster oven. Also sprinkle the bottom tray with a little baking soda to eliminate the burnt smell from drippings and crumbs.

Deep Fryer

The gentle abrasive action of baking soda is ideal for cleaning your deep oil fryer. It will also help absorb residual oils and neutralize odors.

Power Clean Your Blender

The best way to clean your blender is to fill it halfway with water and then add 1 teaspoon of baking soda and a single drop of liquid dish detergent. Secure the lid and run the blender for a few seconds. Rinse clean.

Coffee Maker Cleaning

Keep your coffeemaker clean by brewing up a pot of warm water to which ¼ cup of baking soda has been added. Your coffee will taste great if you brew up this mixture on a monthly basis.

43

Coffee Filter Basket

Run your coffee filter basket or permanent filter under your kitchen faucet then sprinkle on a little baking soda. Clean with an old toothbrush.

COUNTERS and CUTTING BOARDS

Baking soda sprinkled on a sponge or dish cloth instantly becomes a mildly abrasive scouring powder that works well to remove stains from your counters and cutting boards.

If you have cuts on your counter tops apply a baking soda paste *(add just enough water to some baking soda to make a paste)* and prepare to be amazed. The same technique also works well on enamel stove tops that have been scratched.

Baking soda is ideal for removing the following stains:

*Coffee

*Tea

*Fruit juice

*Beet juice

*Kool Aid

*Mustard

*Ink from food price stickers

POTS, PANS, and STONEWARE

Baked on Food

Sprinkle baking soda on any pots and pans with baked on food and add hot water. Leave to soak overnight. The food will soften and come loose making cleaning much easier.

Stubborn Burnt Pans

If your pans are a real mess, bring a couple of inches of water to a boil. Turn off the heat and add ½ cup baking soda. Leave to sit overnight. It should clean up easily in the morning.

Scratched Stoneware

To make the scratches on stoneware less visible, apply a thick paste of baking soda and water and let sit for a few minutes before washing as normal.

Remove Tea Stains

Rid your teapot of stains by filling the pot with hot water and ½ cup baking soda and leave to sit overnight. In the morning, wipe clean and rinse.

GLASS and PLASTIC

Water Bottles

Hot water and baking soda left overnight in your water bottles will remove any stale odors.

Shine Crystal

Make good crystal sparkle by soaking in baking soda and warm water. Rinse and dry.

Clean Vinegar and Oil Cruets

Pour in some baking soda, shake and allow the baking soda to absorb the oils in the bottle. Rinse clean.

Odor-Free Bowls

If you have a plastic bowl with a lid that still smells a little stale after washing add a little baking soda. Before drying, dust the interior of the bowl as you would a cake pan and cover with its' lid. Leave to sit overnight. In the morning, shake off the excess and wipe the bowl clean with a damp cloth.

46

KEEPING IT HANDY

Shaker Style

Pour some baking soda into a handy shaker. Grated cheese shakers work well.

Decorative Bowl

Keep baking soda handy by putting some in a decorative bowl by your sink.

FLOORS

Remove Scuff Marks

Remove scuff marks with a paste of baking soda and water.

Clean Up Grease Spills

Sprinkle a little baking soda on grease spills and wipe with a warm, damp cloth.

Remove Rust

Use a paste of baking soda and water to remove rust stains from floors.

Drain Cleaner – Recipe #1

To clear a clogged drain pour ½ cup each of baking soda and salt down the drain followed by 1 cup of boiling water. Leave to sit overnight and then flush with hot water in the morning. *(See Recipe #2 under 'Cleaning with Vinegar and Baking Soda')*

BAKING SODA TIPS

Keep Sinks and Dishwashers Fresh

Before going on vacation, pour a little baking soda down the kitchen drain and disposal as well as the inside of your dishwasher. Leave your dishwasher open a crack and you won't come home to any stale odors.

Shine Your Sink

Remove hard water stains from your sink and faucets with a paste of baking soda and toothpaste. If the stains are tough use an old toothbrush. Rinse clean.

Deodorize Your Garbage Can

Sprinkle a little baking soda on the bottom of your garbage can, put in a fresh bag and then sprinkle in a little more so it helps absorb any odors until you change the bag again.

Rubber Glove Maintenance

Keep your rubber gloves dry, smelling fresh and easy to slide on by sprinkling a little baking soda on the inside.

No More Rusty Steel Wool

To ward against rust, store steel wool scouring pads in a container filled with baking soda and water immediately after using.

Keep Dish Cloths and Tea Towels Fresh

The best way to keep dish towels fresh between laundering is to sprinkle on a little baking soda. Shake off the excess baking soda in the sink and hang to dry. Wipe your sink with your dish cloth, rinse, and leave to dry.

Make the Most of Old Baking Soda

Don't throw out the baking soda you remove from your fridge and freezer every three months, instead store it with the rest of your cleaning supplies and use it for drain cleaning purposes.

Vinegar Uses

IN THE KITCHEN

Cleaning Your Coffee Maker

If you're looking to remove mineral deposits from your coffee maker use white vinegar. Fill the water reservoir with 1 cup or more of vinegar and run it through a whole cycle. Run it once or twice more with plain water to rinse clean.

Tea Kettle Cleaning

Get rid of mineral deposits in your tea kettle by adding 1/2 cup white vinegar and filling the rest of the kettle with water. Leave to sit overnight. If the mineral deposits are really built up you may want to boil full-strength white vinegar in the kettle a few minutes then let cool before rinsing with plain water.

Can Opener Cleaning

Clean the wheel of a can opener with a toothbrush and a little white vinegar.

Rid Oven Cleaning Odor

To avoid the smell that lingers when you heat up a newly cleaned oven, simply use a sponge soaked in diluted white vinegar for the final rinse.

Remove Strong Odors

Rinse glass jars you want to reuse with a half and half mixture of vinegar and water to remove garlic or other strong odors.

Clean the Garbage Disposal

Use vinegar ice cubes to clean your garbage disposal. Freeze vinegar in two ice cube trays and then run the cubes down the disposal while flushing with cold water. *(Don't forget to rinse the trays out well before making regular ice cubes.)*

FLOORS

Shine Up No-Wax Floors

No-wax floors are best cleaned with a solution of 1 cup vinegar per pail of hot water.

Clean Hardwood Floors

Wash hardwood floors by adding one capful of vinegar to one pail of hot water. Be sure to squeeze out your cloth or mop so it's damp not wet. Too much moisture on hardwood floors is never good.

No More Cloudy Glasses

If your glassware is particularly cloudy, wrap paper towels or a cloth dripped in full-strength white vinegar around the inside and outside of the individual glasses. Let sit for an hour or so before rinsing clean.

Remove Lunch Box Odors

Rid your child's lunch box of odors by placing a slice of bread inside that has been soaked in white vinegar. Leave overnight.

Give Sponges and Cloths New Life

Renew sponges and cloths by placing them in a bowl of water and vinegar. Leave to soak overnight.

Cut Fridge Top Grime

Remove the grime from the top of your refrigerator by wiping with a cloth and some white vinegar.

IN THE BATHROOM

Shower Doors

Wipe shower doors down with a sponge soaked in white vinegar. Rinse with water.

Showerheads

Unclog your showerhead by boiling it in ½ cup of vinegar and one liter of water for five minutes. If the showerhead is plastic, soak in vinegar and hot water instead. If you can't remove the showerhead, pour a solution of warm water and vinegar in a plastic bag and secure over the showerhead with a rubber band. Let soak for an hour.

VINEGAR TIPS

Ward Against Ants

Spray vinegar along doorways, windowsills, countertops and anywhere ants are likely to appear.

Eliminate Sink Odors

Pour a cup or more of vinegar down your kitchen sink. Don't rinse out for at least an hour.

Clean Stained Hands

Remove fruit juice stains from your hands by pouring on a little vinegar and rubbing together before rinsing.

Did You Burn Dinner?

If you want to get rid of the burnt smell from an over-cooked dinner simply boil some water with several teaspoonfuls of vinegar in it for a few minutes.

Shine Sink Fixtures

If your kitchen faucet has a buildup of lime, treat it with a paste made of 2 tablespoons salt and 1 teaspoon white distilled vinegar.

Cleaning Power

KITCHEN CLEANING

Green Clean

To clean your oven the green way, try a combination of baking soda, vinegar, a durable scrubbing pad and lots of elbow grease.

General Appliance Cleaner

A great solution for washing down the exteriors of your appliances is to mix ¼ cup of baking soda with ½ cup of white vinegar and adding to a pail of hot water. For tough cleaning jobs add 1 cup of ammonia.

Deep Clean Cutting Boards

Give your cutting boards a deep clean on a regular basis by sprinkling a little baking soda over the surface and pouring on some vinegar. Once the bubbles have done their thing, rinse the boards with hot water. In addition to keeping your cutting boards free of contamination, the baking soda will also remove intense food odors like onion and garlic.

Baked on Grease

If baked on grease is the issue, pour on equal amounts of baking soda and vinegar and let sit overnight. Wash as usual in the morning.

Eliminate Stale Odors

Clean plastic food storage containers with a combination of hot water and baking soda. If the odor lingers, leave the container to soak overnight in a baking soda and water mixture to which you've also added a little vinegar and dish detergent.

Shine Up Copper Pots

Give new life to copper pots by sprinkling on some baking soda followed by vinegar. Let the pots stand for 15 minutes then rinse clean or polish with half a lemon. Dry.

Need a Better Scouring Cleanser?

Need a good scouring cleanser for kitchen and bathroom cleaning? Combine 1/4 cup baking soda with 1 tablespoon liquid detergent. Add just enough white vinegar to give the paste a thick but creamy texture.

Drain Cleaner - Recipe #2

Open a clogged drain by pouring in 1 cup of baking soda followed by 1 cup of hot vinegar. *(Heat the vinegar in the microwave.)* Wait a few minutes and then flush with hot water. Repeat if necessary. *(See Recipe #1 under 'Baking Soda Uses')*

GETTING RID OF ODORS

Deodorize the Garbage Disposal

Pour 1/2 cup baking soda and 1/2 cup hot white vinegar down your garbage disposal. Let sit for 20 minutes then run some hot water down the disposal.

Rid Your Hands of Odors

If your hands smell of food preparation odors like onions or garlic sprinkle a little baking soda in the palm of one hand and then add just enough water to make a paste. Rub the paste between your hands and rinse off. Pouring some vinegar on your hands usually does an equally good job depending on the odor.

Spring Cleaning
Your Garage

Is your car in the garage or is it in the driveway because the garage is full of stuff? If you've lived in your home for several years and you've got kids, chances are it's the latter.

Ideally how would you like to use your garage – to store your car, as a workspace, or an efficient place to store stuff?

Regardless of your end plans for your garage it's usually best to start from scratch. Recruit all able bodied family members and pull everything out into the driveway to get an accurate picture of what you're really dealing with.

Get Boxes

If you think you'll have a considerable amount of stuff you'd be willing to part with, stop by a grocery store the day before to get some sturdy boxes for organizing what you'll be giving away or selling in a garage sale.

Create Three Piles

Separate everything into one of three piles – what goes back in the garage, items destined for the landfill, and things too good to be thrown out but no longer needed.

Divide and Conquer

Carefully sort through your stuff looking for any items that are damaged, have missing pieces etc. Discard anything that's broken. Group like things together e.g. sporting gear in one spot, auto repair supplies in another.

Storage Bins

Large stackable clear plastic storage containers are your best bet for things like camping gear and seasonal decorations. Use lockable bins for power tools and other dangerous or valuable items. To keep things simple and easy to find, color code the containers used to store the belongings of individual family members. Consider plastic organizers with multiple compartments for storing a variety of similar items you want to keep together.

Wall Storage

Your main options are to either attach shelves or cabinets to your garage walls or put up freestanding units. Either way you'll want to take into account the depth if you're planning on parking your car inside the garage as well. If you find you have little room once your car is in the garage, consider using the available space you do have on the three walls above the height of your car roof.

Try to avoid the temptation of putting things back into your garage before you have acquired the appropriate shelving and storage bins. Speaking of storage bins, you don't have to go out and buy expensive ones. Things like empty coffee or soup cans can be hung directly on the wall to hold small items like nails and screws. The lids of clear jars can also be secured to the underside of shelves and used for the same purpose. Pegboards are ideal for storing lightweight tools of all shapes and sizes. Use a hook or nail and a permanent marker to outline the individual tools so it's easy to tell at a glance where things go.

The following are some ideas to help improve the functionality and storage space in your garage:

Add Workspace Lighting

If you plan to create a workspace, give some thought to adequate lighting and easily accessible light switches. A corkboard is ideal for keeping paperwork like instructions and blueprints handy but out of the way. Consider adding some hooks as well for keeping drop cloths and rags handy.

Mark Your Spot

Looking to park your car in the same spot each time? Hang a tennis ball from the ceiling so that it just touches your windshield when you pull into the garage and/or create a tire stop by bolting a 2-by-4 to the floor.

Create a Storage Loft

A thick piece of plywood positioned in the rafters along with a side ladder running up the wall is all you need to create a simple storage loft. Another option if you're really pressed for space is to build a low storage platform just above the height of your car roof.

Store Flat Items on Walls

Flat items like folding lawn chairs, rakes, and brooms take up little space and can hang directly on the walls.

Use a Hammock for Storage

If you've got an old hammock you no longer use, hang it up across a corner and use as a handy way to store sports equipment. Make sure it's positioned low enough for easy access.

Turn a Garbage Can into a Tool Cart

Turn a basic heavy-duty plastic garbage can with wheels into a handy gardening cart. Store yard and garden tools like rakes and hoes *(with long handles)* inside and fasten hooks into the side *(or use 'S' hooks around the rim)* to attach smaller hand tools. The key is to balance the load so the cart doesn't tip.

Bike Storage

Bikes are best stored on ceiling hooks along one side of the garage, or directly over the hood of your car. Floor-to-ceiling bike racks are also a good option for a family of cyclists. For families with school age kids, consider storing your children's bikes on more height appropriate hooks so they can easily hang their bikes back up by lifting one wheel at a time.

Ventilated Storage

Since the storage of combustible liquids like gasoline, kerosene, and paint thinner are best stored in a well-ventilated space that is separate from your home, consider storing them in a vented shed if you have one. If not, and you have a yard; erect a small metal, vinyl or wood shed with lots of ventilation. Sheds are also the ideal location for things like your lawn mower, trimmer, and related gardening tools and supplies.

Finally, plan to have a garage sale soon otherwise there's a good chance the things you thought were too good to throw away may find their way back into your garage and that's totally counterproductive.

About the Author

Sherrie Le Masurier is an organizing consultant who after 20 years of marriage and four kids has learned a few things house cleaning, decluttering, organizing and routines.

What she didn't know she turned to her parents and grandparents for some wisdom. Sherrie's maternal grandparents were landlords with multiple rental properties and who prided themselves on hands-on cleaning between tenants.

"It's amazing what one can learn from watching an experienced cleaner put a little elbow grease into a task," says Sherrie.

For more tips and ideas on keeping your home and family better organized visit...

www.SherrieLeMasurier.com

www.home-organizing-made-easy.com

3468859R00035

Printed in Great Britain
by Amazon.co.uk, Ltd.,
Marston Gate.